Paradise on Earth with Words

Paradise on Earth with Words

Collection 1: Oceanic

Eric Scott Grand

Eric Scott Grand has been writing poetry for the last thirty years. He has attended poetry symposiums and recorded songs. His work has been previously published in anthologies. Eric Grand lives and writes by the majestic Pacific Ocean in Carlsbad, California.

All rights reserved. No part of this publication may be reproduced, distributed, or transmitted in any form by any means, including photocopying, recording, or other electronic methods without the prior written permission of the author, except in the case of brief quotations embodied in reviews and certain other noncommercial uses permitted by copyright law. For permission requests, write to the author at the address below.

Copyright © 2021 Eric Scott Grand

ericvonnoir@aol.com

ISBN 979-8-218-30810-0

Edited and designed by Tell Tell Poetry

Printed in the United States of America

First Printing, 2021

To my uncle, without whom I would never have experienced my times on the high seas.

Contents

Waterfront	1
Summer	2
Island Hideaway	3
Cove	4
Coast	5
Seagulls	6
A Breeze by the Sea	7
Pelicans	8
Bay	9
Glare Reflection	10
Sunset Palm	11
Beach	12
Bikini	13
Mermaid Maiden	14
Wave	15
Surfer Girl	16
Pipeline	17
Surfers	18
Marine Land	19
Great White Shark	20

Acknowledgments

To all the people involved in the publication of this collection: thank you.

Waterfront

There's room to look at what is further ahead
To watch near the waterfront where it is allowed
To bring folding chairs to not worry about leaving
In a hurry unless it's mandatory where it can be seen
In person to spend with friends men women kids children
Daughters sons moms fathers with infants adolescents
Relatives to visit that allows if permitted to come by
Near the waterfront where you're able to find a spot
To sit for several minutes to remain at your own pace
To leave when you're ready with no one to tell
Let us go now if not directed so to rest there
If that's what you'll want near the waterfront

You're able to see outwards to relax near the waterfront
That's where you're able to be without difficulty comfortably
To see directly in your sight under the sunlight where
You're able also to walk leaves a trail of tracks near
The waterfront where you are able to see people waterski
That can be combined with aerial stunts near the waterfront

It is where beyond is a horizon to get there looks long
Near the waterfront where it is allowed to sit from a distance
To watch what goes on near the waterfront where it is nice
To read that has clean air to breathe if you decided
To go for a run near the waterfront

Summer

It is the part of the year that seems longer
In summer there's more to do outdoors when
Good times can be enjoyed to never forget
What's experienced leaving memories between
Family friends to have fun in summer it gives
A reason not to sleep early not to be in a hurry
To return home when time is on your side
That makes the night young in summer

It is a heat season when you're able to look your best
With seasonal clothing for the climate weather
That leaves to wonder in summer it is to stay
Hydrated that is good to drink fluids
Stay under cover in summer that is okay
To get rest if your health calls for it that's
Understandable if the weather is hard to handle
It gets unbearable to look for shelter in summer

It is when it is preferable to have a festival
Celebration relax take a vacation not think
Of the weather that is hot in summer where
The heat that comes with it makes the temperature
Rise inside want to cook outside to feel good
Have a barbecue not feel stuffy under the collar
In summer

It is when lite clothing is advisable
With the right diet
To stay healthy have energy
Not be tired in summer

Island Hideaway

A place where excitement begins tension ends
There is a sense of contentment that's present
That is private on an island hideaway there are
Countrysides for long drives with green sceneries
With beautiful landscapes on an island hideaway
There are side streets properties for privacy
There's cold mountain air that is there that looks
Like the forest woods there are ways to pass the time
To go for a ride as a passenger on a motorbike
Where you are able to live to stay
On an island hideaway

An exotic location that can be visited for a vacation
That can seem like paradise on an island hideaway
There are ways to escape in a tropical place
There's ways to get exercise that builds stamina
For plenty of energy there are places to wine dine
That allow formal dress there are workshops
For self-improvement festivals that take place
On a weekly basis on an island hideaway there
Are outdoor markets that sell food produce like fruits
That are regional centers to know the area better
There are tour guides to show you the sights
There are areas to rest for overnight guests
There's places to make conversation
On an island hideaway

A popular spot for tourists to get away
On an island hideaway with many activities
To keep busy that you'll prefer that are diverse
To learn to feel good it's a stress-free environment
On an island hideaway where there's an opportunity
To ride double-decker buses there's entertainment
Where people in attendance can participate there
Can be contest prizes that can be a complete surprise
On an island hideaway

Cove

It's where it's remote that's off-road is a cove
Somewhere to explore more once in it's dim
After entered wherever you are able to go
For safety it is better to be careful to watch
Your step to prevent from falling over an edge
If you are distracted in case there is a hole
In a cove it is safer to not go by yourself
For any chance you are not able to trace back
Your tracks to find your way out with the help
Of someone else to have greater odds both
Will find your way out from a cove

It's built into a boulder where it gets cold it is in a cove
Where you're able to go further in deep that water may
Leak if there's moist areas there are parts that are not
Accessible it is not fit to live there could be caverns
That are abandoned if gone alone in a cove the ground
May be unstable that is breakable gravel debris
Can fall easily once stepped on it feels delicate
So that you will need to crouch that the weight
Will not seem heavy makes it appear the height
Is low in a cove

It has a crevice that leads to an entrance that looks
Eroded in a cove that can be investigated to excavate
That can have many entryways to continue into it
That you're able to go in a cove it could be dangerous
Unaware what could be in there with no insulation
The temperature can drop dramatically that it can end up
Frozen in a cove

Coast

It's where objects can float on the coast
Traveling it can take some time that's
A great length by boat on the coast
Ships set sail quick when there is more
Wind that makes it blow in people's faces
There is a sprinkle it produces like rain
If it is too much it can leave
Soak on the coast

It's where dry land meets the brink
That heavy items sink low it is the coast
If gone further down southbound once
You are out far it is hard to navigate
In the direction to go straight it's easy
To get lost without navigational tools
To arrive where you are supposed to
Can be hard if you're not
Knowledgeable in nautical
If not sure which way to go
There's much more to explore on the coast
There could be artifacts that have sunk under
It can be rewarding a surprise that could
Be brought up to the surface it could be
A discovery that has a value
Worth on the coast

It's where lite items stay level at even flow
Is the coast that has a water source for natural
Resources mammals for the use of food clothes
Like shoes products for sale like fragrance
For the most part to show it is the coast
It can be adventurous when it gets treacherous
At the same time dangerous if overcome
It can makes you courageous a cautionary
Measure would be not to fall overboard
On the coast

Seagulls

They gather around when there are clouds
They are seagulls they make sound
Over the ground like crows when
They feel territorial they call others
Alike for help when they feel threatened
There are several wherever they go
When they are not alone they have flown
Where it can get cold they are seagulls
They have a coat that is white with a shade
Of grey they flock where they can huddle
They are seagulls

They enjoy where it's oceanic that is where
They dwell they're seagulls they adapt to their climate
Environment they find shelter where they do not
Swelter they are prone to go where it gets a bit
Under the weather they prefer to be near where
It's watery not muggy when someone throws
Breadcrumbs they want some there are many
The foods they eat are raw they're seagulls
There are most where it gets soak they seem to be
Where it's damp they appear when a storm is near
After rain falls they are seagulls

There are more when the temperature is low
They are seagulls they stand on light posts to see
What is below to have a nice view of what's overhead
In the distance for a period they can be gone
In an instant without a second's notice they can fly
They have a tendency to be where it's windy their size
Is not that small they are seagulls there could be
Amounts found in car lots for food consumption
They can coexist where there's more of a mist
When they see each other in trouble they follow
They're seagulls

A Breeze by the Sea

When the air gets clean that makes it easier to breathe
A breeze by the sea after the fog rolls in
To rinse off what keeps it from being fresh
Completely then the sky is clear by a breeze
By the sea where it can be felt
By locals in their neighborhood
With visitors there for leisure
To inhale what is provided by
A breeze by the sea

When the marine layer is heavy the wind picks up
That leaves a breeze by the sea then eventually
It moves on to another area that won't have moisture
To create a breeze by the sea where natives with their
Relatives stay for recreation to feel at ease near
A breeze by the sea

When the humidity pressure rises it forces
To feel not see a breeze by the sea that pushes
Clouds that look thick then there's precipitation
Of rain to wash away then ultimately it goes in
Another direction that can make it be a breeze by the sea
Where it can be experienced by those
Who live and visit this area
With a breeze by the sea

Pelicans

They fly in unison they are pelicans
Along an area they can be seen
Flapping their wings as much as they can
They are pelicans while in midair
They drop to lower altitudes to eat
What they please to catch snatch
Scoop their food to chew while they have
An aerial view of what is below them
They are pelicans

They take flight sometimes aligned above
They are pelicans they're species that can
Be seen at beaches when they're not close
To shore they could be in the sky soaring
Have sharp beaks that can mostly be seen
In numbers when it's sunny when they're
In squad formations usually a higher elevation
Sometimes over sand they are pelicans
At low level they can scan what they want
To grab a snack they are pelicans

They have flown in sync overhead
They're pelicans that can be seen in the heat
Near the sea where they go that a breeze
Blows in a direction where they can get fish
To eat feast that they bite to nourish their appetite
Fast they are pelicans they glide on the coastline
Inches away where they can bathe find space
Where their bodies can lay on an area
That is wide in diameter that has water
Where they land they are pelicans

Bay

It is part of a section broken off
That takes up a space overlooking a bay
To be temporarily that's made to spend time
Together where to gather take pictures snap
Shots with a smile on your face overlooking
A bay memories can last to reflect on the past
To share your feelings about what you are seeing
That can strike up a conversation of a location seen
Above a ravine that is a short trip to visit with
Your directions to point the way to the place
Overlooking a bay

Its portion is separate apart where a period of time
It's allowed to stay overlooking a bay near the sea
To arrive with friends family that can be a memorable
Moment to get away overlooking a bay that can be
Where to meet if you wanted to speak privately
It has a cutoff point before it reaches an end
To continue further will require a boat with a motor
A paddle a sail overlooking a bay

It is a piece of land where you are able to go alone
If it is permitted it is okay overlooking a bay to see
Briefly with company to walk around the weather
Gets cool there is a beautiful view that can be clear
If it is in the light of day overlooking a bay that
Can serve as inspiration when gathering thoughts
Creating images in your head to be captured in detail
Descriptions to draw paint write
Overlooking a bay

Glare Reflection

It makes the ocean surface shine in a forward
Direction it's a glare reflection by the hours of time
It's formed when it's warm on a clear day to see
While in water wet to feel its effect
Of a glare reflection beyond what is above
It can be seen when it's sunny it glistens in the light
It emits a radiant brilliance it's a glare reflection

Over the sea it's easier to see from a distance
It's a glare reflection within minutes takes place
Near the middle of the day it can be better seen
When the sky is without cloud cover that would prevent
A glare reflection it gets to its height when it shows
A reflective glow that can be seen below
That's shiny where it's watery that can appear
In an instant it's a glare reflection

Across a body of water it can be seen farther distant
It's a glare reflection it gleams in a bright streak
Then ember color shows its wonders that's spectacular
As the sun descends rays of light spread overhead
That at times it can look red like a lit flare it's a glare
Reflection from afar it creates a scenery
That can leave memories near evening
When it gets late it radiates in the air
It's a glare reflection

Sunset Palm

Tides are high you're on my side the sound is calm
In sunset palm around here there are trees a breeze
Waves make a splash there are brunette dudettes
Gorgeous female blonds the sound is calm in sunset palm
Shells cover a moist section hobbyists gather a collection
There is plenty of space this is an ample place
On the coastal basin the sound is calm in sunset palm

Cloud cover is up you're not that far the sound is calm
In sunset palm close it's misty it cannot be seen clearly
Water sounds like thunder makes you watch in wonder
There's early morning haze that makes you see ahead
In a daze that feels numb the sound is calm in sunset palm
Sand fills up land towels support your back you're able
To place an umbrella for shade to be safe if not decided
To sunbathe when it's hot the sound is calm in sunset palm

Temperature is on the rise you're nearby the sound is calm
In sunset palm in the general area is fresh air tropical weather
It gets bright clear as light then starts where it first gets near
Dark where you're able to find a comfortable spot the sound
Is calm in sunset palm visitors find an area to rest where they
Can lie before it's empty that can accommodate many it's serene
The sky can get clear the sound is calm in sunset palm

Beach

The surf the sand the palm trees
Not far from my reach is the beach
Rescue workers surfers a port
It has its share of sports that are extreme
Not far from my reach is the beach current swells
A pier where I get wet feet not far
From my reach is the beach

The shore the wharf the reef
Not far from my reach is the beach
Riptides lifeguards ships dock
There are areas that are deep not far
From my reach is the beach boards stay afloat
Sometimes it's cold where I get soaked knees
Not far from my reach is the beach

The coast the ocean the sea
Not far from my reach is the beach
Safety crews typhoons marinas tsunamis
Early fog later it can be hot cloud cover
Over water that forms near not far
From my reach is the beach there are
Triathlon competitive events that are strenuous
Where I get a drenched body not far
From my reach is the beach

Bikini

It's a two-piece item when put on women
I'm excited that looks good on females
That are ladies in a bikini it's worn to be
Close to the sea to rest comfortably
That looks good on females that are ladies
In a bikini it's fit to swim that makes
Appear skinny that looks good on females
That are ladies in a bikini

It is made of cloth that has a price value cost
That looks good on females that are ladies
In a bikini it's worn to be close to the ocean
To prevent getting burned put on lotion
It covers body parts for comfort that looks good
On females that are ladies in a bikini
That appears relaxed for the back
That looks good on females that are ladies
In a bikini

It comes in a pair to wear that looks good
On females that are ladies in a bikini
It's worn when gone to the coast
To show a body tone that looks good
On females that are ladies in a bikini
To make casual be natural for less tension
That appears loose that looks good on females
That are ladies in a bikini

Mermaid Maiden

A damsel half fish half human part
Woman this mermaid maiden
Her hair is golden blond with braids
She's special in her own way this mermaid
Maiden when she was created they put
Every inch of her body in the right place and
Didn't miss any spots there's no one on earth
Like her this mermaid maiden

She's a feminine amphibian she's a crossbreed
Who lives in the sea when pursued she's
Sensitive this mermaid maiden when she
Shifts her fins she's quick when she needs to
Pick up speed to go deep further she
Explores more when she's near the ocean floor
She can swerve at ease her body at a depth
Where it's hard to get this mermaid maiden she
Can move swiftly easily leaving a splash to go
Where she wants in a dash fast where she stays
Wet this mermaid maiden

A lady of nature with features that are aquatic
Where she's placed that's how she remains this
Mermaid maiden who has qualities based on
Fantasies brought to reality who can be
Submerged where it can be her domain this
Mermaid maiden how she was made captures the
Imagination of storytellers tales fables that
Have been said to enjoy for all ages of this
Mermaid maiden

Wave

It goes one way then ends washed away
It is a wave it slams on impact when it comes
It can make you run it begins with an even flow further
It grows then picks up speed at a high rate
It is a wave that can be dodged when swum under
It can be avoided from below at the right
Moment when it is about to break it is a wave

It is headed in one direction then winds up in another
That is first raised it is a wave when close it sounds
Explosive that gives a fair warning when to evade
It is a wave that gets stronger with wind before it comes
With full force it is better to react than to wait it is a wave

It moves from back to forth it is calm first
Then gets to a height like jumping on a trampoline
That's elevated it is a wave your body weight can handle it
Better from behind when coming in contact at a rapid pace
It is a wave it can clear what is in its path fast that has
A movement that sways it is a wave

Surfer Girl

She looks cute in a wet suit that is accompanied
By seawater she is a surfer girl resting on a surface
That covers her body length with strength she gets up
Quick aware the space she occupies is slick
Who is pushed with a surge she is a surfer girl
Who scurries over rock quarries to get where she wants
In a hurry to practice the skills she knows
She is a surfer girl

She looks fantastic in elastic that suits her she is a surfer girl
Who goes up against current swells to feel exhilarated
That can be an avocation also a competitive sport she is
A surfer girl who is in a rush when surf's up if she does not
She will lose her chance to ride a high tide that she prefers
She is a surfer girl

She looks adorable holding a board she is a surfer girl
Who has to face waves with an object that is long
She must hold on to it strong then stand fast
Then pushed forward with a blunt force
She is a surfer girl who runs where she likes
To have fun without trying to get hurt
She is a surfer girl

Pipeline

It starts calmly intact then ends scattered
Flat when you are close by a pipeline it expands
And becomes vast for miles long it can last with no end
In sight it is a pipeline it grabs anything in its path
Like a clenched fist it has a tight grip
Rather than a hold it bursts its temperature
Can be cool some turn out huge looking over
It is high it is a pipeline

It continues in a rolling motion to get a good height
It is a pipeline where you're swept away higher
Than before when it reaches its peak to end on a surface floor
It makes a crash when it is headed in your direction fast
That can be from behind it is a pipeline it is difficult to say
The effect it will make without warning in a hurry
When it is about to hit less likely it will miss
When there is nowhere to hide it is a pipeline

It will go on in spiral movements it spins before it is finished
Fast until it reaches land that expands to a large mass
That it widens its size it is a pipeline anything in its sight
Is swept away then pulled back into place wind propels it
To reach close to land the result leaves wetness that takes
A while to dry it's a pipeline it loops over and creates
A tunnel then drains like a funnel in a way to recede
Near the sea that leaves a soaked terrain
That looks bright it is a pipeline

Surfers

It is their devotion that keeps them in motion
They stay close to shore they are surfers
They wait to ride with patience before they react
Quickly to stand maintaining their balance
They do their best when they are focused
They are surfers they have a watchful eye
That will not slip by when they're done
Parts of their bodies are wet they are surfers

They use arms hands like paddles
Their feet legs to go over waves upwards
They are surfers on a board their weight
Is supported that is not always easy to keep
Your footing from above the difficulty it is slippery
If you're not able to hold your composure
It is possible not to flip over on their toes
They're able to have control they are surfers
There are ripples that can cause trouble
It is a rush that can happen in an instant
That they encounter close they are surfers

It is their passion that requires action they remain
Near where it is shallow to not get hurt they are surfers
While they stay steady till they get ready then get up
In a hurry before they can get to dry land it takes a lot
Of effort to be better expert surfers they have to look out
Not to get wiped out they have to see clearly
If their vision gets blurry after it gets watery
It keeps them alert they are surfers

Marine Land

Its surface is filled with sand in the marine land
There are aquatic animals that are quick to maneuver
Around obstacles they can handle there is much to explore
If not seen before you are able to breathe easier deeper
With enough oxygen tanks without a problem in the marine
Land where you're able to see amphibian life
For the most part objects feel heavier when raised
By hooks and wire straps in the marine land

Its terrain is saturated it is hard to hold your breath for long
It is the marine land where you're going to need diving gear
To go further lower the inhabitants that occupy it can be hard
To see if you're not equipped with the proper eyewear
You're able to swim far in the marine land where the ground
Is dense that makes it sensitive to touch that whatever felt
Reacts fast a slight tap will do that in the marine land

Its ground bottom is covered much in the marine land
You're able to stay at a certain depth with the proper
Equipment it's possible to stay longer underwater
As much as you possibly can in the marine land
There's transportation that you will need a lot of patience
To get to a destination with the use of tools for navigation
In the direction it pointed in the marine land

Great White Shark

It has gills it hardly stays still its teeth
Are sharp it is a great white shark
It bites it has a voracious appetite
When it reaches the ocean surface it makes
Most people nervous it has a cold heart
It's a great white shark I wouldn't want
To be in its way when it's out for prey
When divers are lowered underwater in a cage
It vents its rage I would not want to confront
A great white shark

It has fins it swims and rarely stops it is
A great white shark it can devour in less
Than an hour a chunk of meat quickly
That it munches it is a great white shark
It is heavy to carry it is restless and it becomes
Territorial I would not like to encounter a
Great white shark

It breathes in the sea that does not cease
It's hard to catch it is a great white shark
For a meal it is nutritious a species it is vicious
When it gets near shore there are warning alerts
So there will be no harm from a great white shark
They stir the nerves when they go in circles
When they're tapped they snap that is a confrontation
That's dangerous I would not like to come in contact
With a great white shark

www.ingramcontent.com/pod-product-compliance
Lightning Source LLC
Chambersburg PA
CBHW022027050526
44107CB00096B/30